50 Decadent Cake Layer Recipes

By: Kelly Johnson

Table of Contents

- Classic Red Velvet Cake
- Triple Chocolate Mousse Cake
- Lemon Raspberry Layer Cake
- Carrot Cake with Cream Cheese Frosting
- Salted Caramel Chocolate Cake
- Coconut Cream Cake
- Strawberry Shortcake Layer Cake
- Vanilla Bean and Almond Cake
- Coffee Hazelnut Cake
- Funfetti Celebration Cake
- Pumpkin Spice Layer Cake
- Chocolate Fudge Cake
- Coconut Lime Cake
- Black Forest Cake
- Lemon Blueberry Cake
- S'mores Layer Cake
- Tiramisu Cake
- Peach Almond Cake
- Strawberry Champagne Cake
- Chocolate Peanut Butter Cake
- Red Wine Chocolate Cake
- Mocha Cake with Espresso Buttercream
- Raspberry Almond Cake
- Spiced Apple Layer Cake
- Maple Pecan Cake
- Pina Colada Layer Cake
- Almond Joy Layer Cake
- Pistachio Rose Cake
- Chocolate Mint Cake
- Vanilla Bean and Caramel Cake
- White Chocolate Raspberry Cake
- Banana Foster Cake
- Coconut Pineapple Cake
- Toffee Caramel Cake
- Lemon Poppy Seed Cake

- Chocolate Orange Cake
- Mint Chocolate Chip Cake
- Churro Layer Cake
- Chai Spice Layer Cake
- Dulce de Leche Cake
- Bourbon Pecan Cake
- Cookies and Cream Cake
- Key Lime Pie Cake
- Apple Cinnamon Cake
- Cherry Almond Cake
- Cherry Blossom Cake
- Gingerbread Spice Cake
- Blueberry Cream Cheese Cake
- Maple Brown Sugar Cake
- Tropical Mango Coconut Cake

Classic Red Velvet Cake

Ingredients

For the Cake:

- 2 ½ cups (310g) all-purpose flour
- 1 ½ cups (300g) granulated sugar
- 1 tsp baking soda
- 1 tsp cocoa powder
- 1 tsp salt
- 1 ½ cups (360ml) vegetable oil
- 2 large eggs
- 1 cup (240ml) buttermilk
- 2 tbsp (30ml) red food coloring
- 1 tsp vanilla extract
- 1 tsp white vinegar

For the Frosting:

- 8 oz (225g) cream cheese, softened
- ½ cup (115g) unsalted butter, softened
- 4 cups (480g) powdered sugar
- 1 tsp vanilla extract

Instructions

1. **Prepare the Cake:**
   - Preheat the oven to 350°F (175°C). Grease and line two 9-inch (23cm) round cake pans.
   - In a large bowl, whisk together flour, sugar, baking soda, cocoa powder, and salt.
   - In another bowl, beat together oil, eggs, buttermilk, food coloring, vanilla, and vinegar. Gradually add the dry ingredients and mix until smooth.
   - Divide the batter between the pans and bake for 25-30 minutes. Let cool completely.
2. **Prepare the Frosting:**
   - Beat cream cheese and butter until smooth and creamy. Gradually add powdered sugar and vanilla extract. Beat until fluffy.
3. **Assemble the Cake:**
   - Frost the cooled cake layers with the cream cheese frosting.

Triple Chocolate Mousse Cake

Ingredients

For the Cake:

- 1 ¾ cups (220g) all-purpose flour
- 1 tsp baking powder
- ½ tsp salt
- 1 cup (200g) granulated sugar
- ½ cup (115g) unsalted butter, softened
- 2 large eggs
- 1 tsp vanilla extract
- 1 cup (240ml) whole milk
- 4 oz (115g) dark chocolate, melted

For the Mousse Layers:

- 4 oz (115g) dark chocolate, chopped
- 4 oz (115g) milk chocolate, chopped
- 4 oz (115g) white chocolate, chopped
- 2 cups (480ml) heavy cream
- 3 tbsp powdered sugar
- 1 tsp vanilla extract

Instructions

1. **Prepare the Cake:**
   - Preheat the oven to 350°F (175°C). Grease and line two 9-inch (23cm) round cake pans.
   - In a bowl, whisk together flour, baking powder, and salt.
   - In another bowl, beat together butter and sugar until light and fluffy. Add eggs one at a time, then stir in vanilla extract. Gradually add flour mixture, alternating with milk, until smooth. Fold in melted dark chocolate.
   - Divide the batter between the pans and bake for 20-25 minutes. Let cool.
2. **Prepare the Mousse Layers:**
   - In separate bowls, melt the dark, milk, and white chocolates over a double boiler. Whisk the cream and powdered sugar in a chilled bowl until stiff peaks form, then divide the whipped cream between the chocolate mixtures. Gently fold the whipped cream into each chocolate, creating three separate mousse mixtures.

3. **Assemble the Cake:**
    - Layer the cakes with dark chocolate mousse, milk chocolate mousse, and white chocolate mousse. Chill in the fridge until set.

Lemon Raspberry Layer Cake

Ingredients

For the Cake:

- 2 cups (250g) all-purpose flour
- 1 tsp baking powder
- ½ tsp baking soda
- ¼ tsp salt
- 1 cup (200g) granulated sugar
- ½ cup (115g) unsalted butter, softened
- 2 large eggs
- 1 tsp vanilla extract
- 1 cup (240ml) buttermilk
- Zest of 1 lemon
- 1 cup (150g) fresh raspberries

For the Frosting:

- 8 oz (225g) cream cheese, softened
- ½ cup (115g) unsalted butter, softened
- 4 cups (480g) powdered sugar
- 2 tbsp lemon juice
- 1 tsp vanilla extract
- ½ cup (75g) fresh raspberries for garnish

Instructions

1. **Prepare the Cake:**
    - Preheat the oven to 350°F (175°C). Grease and line two 9-inch (23cm) round cake pans.
    - In a bowl, whisk together flour, baking powder, baking soda, and salt.
    - In a separate bowl, beat together butter and sugar until fluffy. Add eggs one at a time, then stir in vanilla extract and lemon zest. Gradually add the dry ingredients, alternating with buttermilk, until smooth. Gently fold in raspberries.
    - Divide the batter between the pans and bake for 25-30 minutes. Let cool completely.
2. **Prepare the Frosting:**

    - Beat together cream cheese and butter until smooth. Gradually add powdered sugar, lemon juice, and vanilla extract, beating until fluffy.
3. **Assemble the Cake:**
    - Frost the cooled cake layers with the lemon cream cheese frosting and top with fresh raspberries.

Carrot Cake with Cream Cheese Frosting

Ingredients

For the Cake:

- 2 cups (250g) all-purpose flour
- 1 ½ tsp baking powder
- 1 tsp baking soda
- ½ tsp salt
- 2 tsp ground cinnamon
- 1 ½ cups (300g) granulated sugar
- 1 cup (240ml) vegetable oil
- 4 large eggs
- 2 tsp vanilla extract
- 3 cups (300g) grated carrots
- 1 cup (120g) chopped walnuts (optional)

For the Frosting:

- 8 oz (225g) cream cheese, softened
- ½ cup (115g) unsalted butter, softened
- 4 cups (480g) powdered sugar
- 1 tsp vanilla extract

Instructions

1. **Prepare the Cake:**
    - Preheat the oven to 350°F (175°C). Grease and line two 9-inch (23cm) round cake pans.
    - In a bowl, whisk together flour, baking powder, baking soda, salt, and cinnamon.
    - In a separate bowl, beat together sugar, oil, eggs, and vanilla extract. Gradually add the dry ingredients until smooth. Fold in grated carrots and walnuts (if using).
    - Divide the batter between the pans and bake for 30-35 minutes. Let cool.
2. **Prepare the Frosting:**
    - Beat together cream cheese and butter until smooth. Gradually add powdered sugar and vanilla extract, beating until fluffy.
3. **Assemble the Cake:**
    - Frost the cooled cake layers with cream cheese frosting.

Salted Caramel Chocolate Cake

Ingredients

For the Cake:

- 1 ¾ cups (220g) all-purpose flour
- 1 tsp baking powder
- 1 tsp baking soda
- ¼ tsp salt
- 1 cup (200g) granulated sugar
- ½ cup (115g) unsalted butter, softened
- 2 large eggs
- 1 tsp vanilla extract
- 1 cup (240ml) milk
- ½ cup (120g) salted caramel sauce
- 2 tbsp cocoa powder

For the Frosting:

- 1 ½ cups (360ml) heavy cream
- 1 cup (240g) semi-sweet chocolate chips
- 2 tbsp salted caramel sauce

Instructions

1. **Prepare the Cake:**
    - Preheat the oven to 350°F (175°C). Grease and line two 9-inch (23cm) round cake pans.
    - In a bowl, whisk together flour, baking powder, baking soda, salt, and cocoa powder.
    - In another bowl, beat together butter and sugar until light and fluffy. Add eggs one at a time, then stir in vanilla extract and salted caramel sauce.
    - Gradually add the dry ingredients, alternating with milk, until smooth.
    - Divide the batter between the pans and bake for 25-30 minutes. Let cool.
2. **Prepare the Frosting:**
    - Heat heavy cream in a saucepan until it begins to simmer. Pour over chocolate chips and stir until smooth. Stir in salted caramel sauce.
3. **Assemble the Cake:**
    - Frost the cooled cakes with the salted caramel chocolate frosting.

Coconut Cream Cake

Ingredients

For the Cake:

- 2 cups (250g) all-purpose flour
- 1 tsp baking powder
- ½ tsp baking soda
- ¼ tsp salt
- 1 cup (200g) granulated sugar
- ½ cup (115g) unsalted butter, softened
- 2 large eggs
- 1 tsp vanilla extract
- 1 cup (240ml) coconut milk
- 1 cup (100g) shredded coconut

For the Frosting:

- 1 cup (240ml) heavy cream
- 2 cups (240g) powdered sugar
- 1 tsp vanilla extract
- 1 cup (100g) shredded coconut, toasted

Instructions

1. **Prepare the Cake:**
    - Preheat the oven to 350°F (175°C). Grease and line two 9-inch (23cm) round cake pans.
    - In a bowl, whisk together flour, baking powder, baking soda, salt, and shredded coconut.
    - In a separate bowl, beat together butter and sugar until light and fluffy. Add eggs one at a time, then stir in vanilla extract and coconut milk.
    - Gradually add the dry ingredients until smooth. Divide the batter between the pans and bake for 25-30 minutes. Let cool.
2. **Prepare the Frosting:**
    - Beat heavy cream and powdered sugar until stiff peaks form. Stir in vanilla extract.
3. **Assemble the Cake:**
    - Frost the cooled cakes with whipped cream frosting and top with toasted shredded coconut.

Coffee Hazelnut Cake

Ingredients

For the Cake:

- 2 cups (250g) all-purpose flour
- 1 tsp baking powder
- ½ tsp baking soda
- ¼ tsp salt
- ½ cup (115g) unsalted butter, softened
- 1 cup (200g) granulated sugar
- 2 large eggs
- 1 tsp vanilla extract
- 1 cup (240ml) brewed coffee, cooled
- 1 cup (120g) ground hazelnuts

For the Frosting:

- 8 oz (225g) cream cheese, softened
- ½ cup (115g) unsalted butter, softened
- 4 cups (480g) powdered sugar
- 2 tbsp brewed coffee
- 1 tsp vanilla extract
- ½ cup (60g) chopped hazelnuts for garnish

Instructions

1. **Prepare the Cake:**
    - Preheat the oven to 350°F (175°C). Grease and line two 9-inch (23cm) round cake pans.
    - In a bowl, whisk together flour, baking powder, baking soda, and salt.
    - In a separate bowl, beat together butter and sugar until fluffy. Add eggs one at a time, then stir in vanilla extract. Gradually add the dry ingredients, alternating with brewed coffee, until smooth. Fold in ground hazelnuts.
    - Divide the batter between the pans and bake for 25-30 minutes. Let cool.
2. **Prepare the Frosting:**
    - Beat together cream cheese and butter until smooth. Gradually add powdered sugar, coffee, and vanilla extract, beating until fluffy.
3. **Assemble the Cake:**

- Frost the cooled cakes with the coffee cream cheese frosting and top with chopped hazelnuts.

Funfetti Celebration Cake

Ingredients

For the Cake:

- 2 ½ cups (310g) all-purpose flour
- 2 tsp baking powder
- ½ tsp salt
- 1 cup (200g) granulated sugar
- ½ cup (115g) unsalted butter, softened
- 3 large eggs
- 1 tsp vanilla extract
- 1 cup (240ml) buttermilk
- ½ cup (80g) rainbow sprinkles

For the Frosting:

- 1 cup (240g) unsalted butter, softened
- 4 cups (480g) powdered sugar
- 2 tsp vanilla extract
- 2 tbsp heavy cream
- ½ cup (80g) rainbow sprinkles for garnish

Instructions

1. **Prepare the Cake:**
    - Preheat the oven to 350°F (175°C). Grease and line two 9-inch (23cm) round cake pans.
    - In a bowl, whisk together flour, baking powder, and salt.
    - In another bowl, beat together butter and sugar until light and fluffy. Add eggs one at a time, then stir in vanilla extract. Gradually add the dry ingredients, alternating with buttermilk, until smooth. Fold in rainbow sprinkles.
    - Divide the batter between the pans and bake for 25-30 minutes. Let cool.
2. **Prepare the Frosting:**
    - Beat butter until smooth. Gradually add powdered sugar, vanilla extract, and heavy cream, beating until fluffy.
3. **Assemble the Cake:**
    - Frost the cooled cakes with the buttercream frosting and top with rainbow sprinkles.

Pumpkin Spice Layer Cake

Ingredients

For the Cake:

- 2 cups (250g) all-purpose flour
- 1 ½ tsp baking powder
- 1 tsp baking soda
- 1 ½ tsp ground cinnamon
- 1 tsp ground nutmeg
- ½ tsp ground ginger
- ½ tsp salt
- 1 cup (200g) granulated sugar
- ½ cup (115g) unsalted butter, softened
- 3 large eggs
- 1 ½ cups (360g) canned pumpkin puree
- 1 tsp vanilla extract

For the Frosting:

- 8 oz (225g) cream cheese, softened
- ½ cup (115g) unsalted butter, softened
- 4 cups (480g) powdered sugar
- 1 tsp vanilla extract

Instructions

1. **Prepare the Cake:**
    - Preheat the oven to 350°F (175°C). Grease and line two 9-inch (23cm) round cake pans.
    - In a bowl, whisk together flour, baking powder, baking soda, cinnamon, nutmeg, ginger, and salt.
    - In another bowl, beat together butter and sugar until fluffy. Add eggs one at a time, then stir in pumpkin puree and vanilla extract. Gradually add the dry ingredients until smooth.
    - Divide the batter between the pans and bake for 25-30 minutes. Let cool.
2. **Prepare the Frosting:**
    - Beat together cream cheese and butter until smooth. Gradually add powdered sugar and vanilla extract, beating until fluffy.
3. **Assemble the Cake:**

- Frost the cooled cakes with the cream cheese frosting.

Chocolate Fudge Cake

Ingredients

For the Cake:

- 1 ¾ cups (220g) all-purpose flour
- 1 ½ tsp baking powder
- ½ tsp baking soda
- ½ tsp salt
- 1 cup (200g) granulated sugar
- ½ cup (115g) unsalted butter, softened
- 1 cup (240ml) buttermilk
- 2 large eggs
- ½ cup (120g) melted dark chocolate
- 1 tsp vanilla extract

For the Frosting:

- 1 ½ cups (360ml) heavy cream
- 1 cup (240g) semi-sweet chocolate chips
- 2 tbsp unsalted butter

Instructions

1. **Prepare the Cake:**
    - Preheat the oven to 350°F (175°C). Grease and line two 9-inch (23cm) round cake pans.
    - In a bowl, whisk together flour, baking powder, baking soda, and salt.
    - In another bowl, beat together butter and sugar until fluffy. Add eggs one at a time, then stir in buttermilk, melted chocolate, and vanilla extract. Gradually add the dry ingredients until smooth.
    - Divide the batter between the pans and bake for 25-30 minutes. Let cool.
2. **Prepare the Frosting:**
    - Heat the heavy cream in a saucepan until it begins to simmer. Pour over chocolate chips and butter, stirring until smooth.
3. **Assemble the Cake:**
    - Frost the cooled cakes with the chocolate fudge frosting.

Coconut Lime Cake

Ingredients

For the Cake:

- 2 cups (250g) all-purpose flour
- 2 tsp baking powder
- ½ tsp salt
- 1 cup (200g) granulated sugar
- ½ cup (115g) unsalted butter, softened
- 2 large eggs
- 1 tsp vanilla extract
- 1 cup (240ml) coconut milk
- Zest of 2 limes
- 1 cup (100g) shredded coconut

For the Frosting:

- 1 cup (240g) unsalted butter, softened
- 4 cups (480g) powdered sugar
- 2 tbsp lime juice
- 1 tsp vanilla extract
- 1 cup (100g) shredded coconut for garnish

Instructions

1. **Prepare the Cake:**
    - Preheat the oven to 350°F (175°C). Grease and line two 9-inch (23cm) round cake pans.
    - In a bowl, whisk together flour, baking powder, and salt.
    - In another bowl, beat together butter and sugar until light and fluffy. Add eggs one at a time, then stir in vanilla extract, lime zest, and coconut milk. Gradually add the dry ingredients until smooth. Fold in shredded coconut.
    - Divide the batter between the pans and bake for 25-30 minutes. Let cool.
2. **Prepare the Frosting:**
    - Beat together butter, powdered sugar, lime juice, and vanilla extract until smooth.
3. **Assemble the Cake:**
    - Frost the cooled cakes with the lime buttercream frosting and top with shredded coconut.

Black Forest Cake

Ingredients

For the Cake:

- 1 ¾ cups (220g) all-purpose flour
- 1 tsp baking powder
- 1 tsp baking soda
- ½ tsp salt
- 1 cup (200g) granulated sugar
- ½ cup (115g) unsalted butter, softened
- 2 large eggs
- 1 tsp vanilla extract
- 1 cup (240ml) buttermilk
- ½ cup (120g) cocoa powder
- 1 cup (240g) cherry pie filling

For the Frosting:

- 2 cups (480ml) heavy cream
- 4 tbsp powdered sugar
- 1 tsp vanilla extract
- ½ cup (60g) chocolate shavings
- 1 cup (150g) maraschino cherries for garnish

Instructions

1. **Prepare the Cake:**
   - Preheat the oven to 350°F (175°C). Grease and line two 9-inch (23cm) round cake pans.
   - In a bowl, whisk together flour, baking powder, baking soda, salt, and cocoa powder.
   - In another bowl, beat together butter and sugar until light and fluffy. Add eggs one at a time, then stir in vanilla extract and buttermilk. Gradually add the dry ingredients until smooth.
   - Fold in cherry pie filling, then divide the batter between the pans and bake for 25-30 minutes. Let cool.
2. **Prepare the Frosting:**
   - Beat together heavy cream, powdered sugar, and vanilla extract until stiff peaks form.

3. **Assemble the Cake:**
    - Frost the cooled cakes with whipped cream frosting, sprinkle with chocolate shavings, and top with maraschino cherries.

Tiramisu Cake

Ingredients

For the Cake:

- 2 cups (250g) all-purpose flour
- 1 ½ tsp baking powder
- ½ tsp salt
- 1 cup (200g) granulated sugar
- ½ cup (115g) unsalted butter, softened
- 3 large eggs
- 1 tsp vanilla extract
- 1 cup (240ml) brewed espresso, cooled
- 2 tbsp coffee liqueur (optional)

For the Frosting:

- 8 oz (225g) mascarpone cheese, softened
- 1 ½ cups (360ml) heavy cream
- ½ cup (60g) powdered sugar
- 1 tsp vanilla extract
- 2 tbsp cocoa powder for dusting

For the Assembly:

- 1 cup (240ml) brewed espresso, cooled
- 2 tbsp coffee liqueur (optional)

Instructions

1. **Prepare the Cake:**
    - Preheat the oven to 350°F (175°C). Grease and line two 9-inch (23cm) round cake pans.
    - In a bowl, whisk together flour, baking powder, and salt.
    - In another bowl, beat together butter and sugar until fluffy. Add eggs one at a time, then stir in vanilla extract. Gradually add the dry ingredients alternating with brewed espresso until smooth. Fold in coffee liqueur if desired.
    - Divide the batter between the pans and bake for 25-30 minutes. Let cool.
2. **Prepare the Frosting:**

- Beat mascarpone cheese, heavy cream, powdered sugar, and vanilla extract until stiff peaks form.

3. **Assemble the Cake:**
    - Once the cakes have cooled, brush the layers with brewed espresso (and coffee liqueur if desired). Frost the cakes with the mascarpone frosting and dust with cocoa powder.

Peach Almond Cake

Ingredients

For the Cake:

- 2 cups (250g) all-purpose flour
- 1 ½ tsp baking powder
- ¼ tsp salt
- 1 cup (200g) granulated sugar
- ½ cup (115g) unsalted butter, softened
- 3 large eggs
- 1 tsp almond extract
- 1 cup (240g) peach puree (fresh or canned)
- ½ cup (50g) sliced almonds for topping

For the Frosting:

- 8 oz (225g) cream cheese, softened
- ½ cup (115g) unsalted butter, softened
- 4 cups (480g) powdered sugar
- 1 tsp almond extract

Instructions

1. **Prepare the Cake:**
    - Preheat the oven to 350°F (175°C). Grease and line two 9-inch (23cm) round cake pans.
    - In a bowl, whisk together flour, baking powder, and salt.
    - In another bowl, beat together butter and sugar until fluffy. Add eggs one at a time, then stir in almond extract and peach puree. Gradually add the dry ingredients until smooth.
    - Divide the batter between the pans and bake for 25-30 minutes. Let cool.
2. **Prepare the Frosting:**
    - Beat together cream cheese, butter, powdered sugar, and almond extract until smooth.
3. **Assemble the Cake:**
    - Frost the cooled cakes with the almond cream cheese frosting and top with sliced almonds.

Strawberry Champagne Cake

Ingredients

For the Cake:

- 2 cups (250g) all-purpose flour
- 1 ½ tsp baking powder
- ¼ tsp salt
- 1 cup (200g) granulated sugar
- ½ cup (115g) unsalted butter, softened
- 3 large eggs
- 1 tsp vanilla extract
- ½ cup (120ml) champagne
- 1 cup (100g) chopped fresh strawberries

For the Frosting:

- 8 oz (225g) cream cheese, softened
- ½ cup (115g) unsalted butter, softened
- 4 cups (480g) powdered sugar
- 2 tbsp champagne
- Fresh strawberries for garnish

Instructions

1. **Prepare the Cake:**
    - Preheat the oven to 350°F (175°C). Grease and line two 9-inch (23cm) round cake pans.
    - In a bowl, whisk together flour, baking powder, and salt.
    - In another bowl, beat together butter and sugar until fluffy. Add eggs one at a time, then stir in vanilla extract and champagne. Gradually add the dry ingredients, then fold in chopped strawberries.
    - Divide the batter between the pans and bake for 25-30 minutes. Let cool.
2. **Prepare the Frosting:**
    - Beat together cream cheese, butter, powdered sugar, and champagne until smooth.
3. **Assemble the Cake:**
    - Frost the cooled cakes with the champagne cream cheese frosting and garnish with fresh strawberries.

Chocolate Peanut Butter Cake

Ingredients

For the Cake:

- 1 ¾ cups (220g) all-purpose flour
- 1 ½ tsp baking powder
- ½ tsp baking soda
- ½ tsp salt
- 1 cup (200g) granulated sugar
- ½ cup (115g) unsalted butter, softened
- 1 cup (240ml) buttermilk
- 2 large eggs
- ½ cup (120g) peanut butter
- 1 cup (240ml) brewed coffee
- ½ cup (60g) cocoa powder

For the Frosting:

- 1 cup (240g) creamy peanut butter
- ½ cup (115g) unsalted butter, softened
- 4 cups (480g) powdered sugar
- 2 tbsp milk
- 1 tsp vanilla extract

Instructions

1. **Prepare the Cake:**
   - Preheat the oven to 350°F (175°C). Grease and line two 9-inch (23cm) round cake pans.
   - In a bowl, whisk together flour, baking powder, baking soda, salt, and cocoa powder.
   - In another bowl, beat together butter and sugar until fluffy. Add eggs one at a time, then stir in peanut butter and brewed coffee. Gradually add the dry ingredients alternating with buttermilk.
   - Divide the batter between the pans and bake for 25-30 minutes. Let cool.
2. **Prepare the Frosting:**
   - Beat together peanut butter, butter, powdered sugar, milk, and vanilla extract until smooth.
3. **Assemble the Cake:**

- Frost the cooled cakes with the peanut butter frosting.

Red Wine Chocolate Cake

Ingredients

For the Cake:

- 2 cups (250g) all-purpose flour
- 1 ½ tsp baking powder
- ½ tsp baking soda
- 1 tsp salt
- 1 cup (200g) granulated sugar
- ½ cup (115g) unsalted butter, softened
- 2 large eggs
- 1 cup (240ml) red wine (preferably dry red wine)
- 1 cup (120g) cocoa powder
- 1 tsp vanilla extract

For the Frosting:

- 8 oz (225g) cream cheese, softened
- ½ cup (115g) unsalted butter, softened
- 4 cups (480g) powdered sugar
- 2 tbsp red wine

Instructions

1. **Prepare the Cake:**
    - Preheat the oven to 350°F (175°C). Grease and line two 9-inch (23cm) round cake pans.
    - In a bowl, whisk together flour, baking powder, baking soda, salt, and cocoa powder.
    - In another bowl, beat together butter and sugar until fluffy. Add eggs one at a time, then stir in vanilla extract and red wine. Gradually add the dry ingredients until smooth.
    - Divide the batter between the pans and bake for 25-30 minutes. Let cool.
2. **Prepare the Frosting:**
    - Beat together cream cheese, butter, powdered sugar, and red wine until smooth.
3. **Assemble the Cake:**
    - Frost the cooled cakes with the red wine cream cheese frosting.

Mocha Cake with Espresso Buttercream

Ingredients

For the Cake:

- 1 ¾ cups (220g) all-purpose flour
- 1 ½ tsp baking powder
- ½ tsp baking soda
- ½ tsp salt
- 1 cup (200g) granulated sugar
- ½ cup (115g) unsalted butter, softened
- 1 cup (240ml) brewed espresso, cooled
- 2 large eggs
- 1 tsp vanilla extract
- ½ cup (60g) cocoa powder

For the Frosting:

- 1 cup (240g) unsalted butter, softened
- 4 cups (480g) powdered sugar
- 2 tbsp brewed espresso
- 1 tsp vanilla extract

Instructions

1. **Prepare the Cake:**
    - Preheat the oven to 350°F (175°C). Grease and line two 9-inch (23cm) round cake pans.
    - In a bowl, whisk together flour, baking powder, baking soda, salt, and cocoa powder.
    - In another bowl, beat together butter and sugar until fluffy. Add eggs one at a time, then stir in vanilla extract and brewed espresso. Gradually add the dry ingredients until smooth.
    - Divide the batter between the pans and bake for 25-30 minutes. Let cool.
2. **Prepare the Frosting:**
    - Beat together butter, powdered sugar, brewed espresso, and vanilla extract until smooth.
3. **Assemble the Cake:**
    - Frost the cooled cakes with the espresso buttercream.

Maple Pecan Cake

Ingredients

For the Cake:

- 2 cups (250g) all-purpose flour
- 1 ½ tsp baking powder
- ¼ tsp salt
- 1 cup (200g) brown sugar, packed
- ½ cup (115g) unsalted butter, softened
- 2 large eggs
- 1 tsp vanilla extract
- 1 cup (240ml) maple syrup
- 1 cup (100g) chopped pecans

For the Frosting:

- 8 oz (225g) cream cheese, softened
- ¼ cup (60g) unsalted butter, softened
- 4 cups (480g) powdered sugar
- 2 tbsp maple syrup
- 1 tsp vanilla extract

For Garnish:

- Whole pecans for decoration

Instructions

1. **Prepare the Cake:**
    - Preheat the oven to 350°F (175°C). Grease and line two 9-inch (23cm) round cake pans.
    - In a bowl, whisk together flour, baking powder, and salt.
    - In another bowl, beat together brown sugar and butter until creamy. Add eggs one at a time, then stir in vanilla extract and maple syrup.
    - Gradually add the dry ingredients until combined, then fold in chopped pecans.
    - Divide the batter between the pans and bake for 25-30 minutes. Let cool.
2. **Prepare the Frosting:**

- Beat together cream cheese, butter, powdered sugar, maple syrup, and vanilla extract until smooth.

3. **Assemble the Cake:**
    - Frost the cooled cakes with the maple cream cheese frosting and garnish with whole pecans.

Pina Colada Layer Cake

Ingredients

For the Cake:

- 2 cups (250g) all-purpose flour
- 1 ½ tsp baking powder
- ½ tsp salt
- 1 cup (200g) granulated sugar
- ½ cup (115g) unsalted butter, softened
- 2 large eggs
- 1 tsp vanilla extract
- 1 cup (240ml) coconut milk
- ½ cup (120ml) pineapple juice
- 1 cup (100g) shredded coconut
- 1 cup (120g) chopped pineapple (drained)

For the Frosting:

- 8 oz (225g) cream cheese, softened
- ½ cup (115g) unsalted butter, softened
- 4 cups (480g) powdered sugar
- 1 tsp vanilla extract
- 2 tbsp pineapple juice
- Shredded coconut for garnish

Instructions

1. **Prepare the Cake:**
    - Preheat the oven to 350°F (175°C). Grease and line two 9-inch (23cm) round cake pans.
    - In a bowl, whisk together flour, baking powder, and salt.
    - In another bowl, beat together sugar and butter until fluffy. Add eggs one at a time, then stir in vanilla extract.
    - Gradually add coconut milk and pineapple juice, alternating with the dry ingredients. Fold in shredded coconut and chopped pineapple.
    - Divide the batter between the pans and bake for 25-30 minutes. Let cool.
2. **Prepare the Frosting:**
    - Beat together cream cheese, butter, powdered sugar, vanilla extract, and pineapple juice until smooth.

3. **Assemble the Cake:**
    - Frost the cooled cakes with the pineapple cream cheese frosting and garnish with shredded coconut.

Almond Joy Layer Cake

Ingredients

For the Cake:

- 2 cups (250g) all-purpose flour
- 1 ½ tsp baking powder
- ½ tsp baking soda
- ½ tsp salt
- 1 cup (200g) granulated sugar
- ½ cup (115g) unsalted butter, softened
- 2 large eggs
- 1 tsp vanilla extract
- ½ cup (120ml) coconut milk
- 1 cup (100g) shredded coconut
- 1 cup (150g) chopped almonds
- 1 cup (120g) chocolate chips

For the Frosting:

- 8 oz (225g) cream cheese, softened
- ½ cup (115g) unsalted butter, softened
- 4 cups (480g) powdered sugar
- 1 tsp vanilla extract
- ½ cup (120g) chocolate ganache (or melted chocolate)

Instructions

1. **Prepare the Cake:**
    - Preheat the oven to 350°F (175°C). Grease and line two 9-inch (23cm) round cake pans.
    - In a bowl, whisk together flour, baking powder, baking soda, and salt.
    - In another bowl, beat together sugar and butter until fluffy. Add eggs one at a time, then stir in vanilla extract and coconut milk.
    - Gradually add the dry ingredients until combined, then fold in shredded coconut, chopped almonds, and chocolate chips.
    - Divide the batter between the pans and bake for 25-30 minutes. Let cool.
2. **Prepare the Frosting:**
    - Beat together cream cheese, butter, powdered sugar, and vanilla extract until smooth.

        - Gradually add the chocolate ganache or melted chocolate until well incorporated.
3. **Assemble the Cake:**
        - Frost the cooled cakes with the chocolate cream cheese frosting.

Pistachio Rose Cake

Ingredients

For the Cake:

- 2 cups (250g) all-purpose flour
- 1 ½ tsp baking powder
- ¼ tsp salt
- 1 cup (200g) granulated sugar
- ½ cup (115g) unsalted butter, softened
- 2 large eggs
- 1 tsp rose water
- 1 cup (100g) ground pistachios
- ½ cup (120ml) milk

For the Frosting:

- 8 oz (225g) cream cheese, softened
- ½ cup (115g) unsalted butter, softened
- 4 cups (480g) powdered sugar
- 1 tsp rose water
- 1 tbsp pistachio paste or ground pistachios (optional)

For Garnish:

- Crushed pistachios for decoration

Instructions

1. **Prepare the Cake:**
   - Preheat the oven to 350°F (175°C). Grease and line two 9-inch (23cm) round cake pans.
   - In a bowl, whisk together flour, baking powder, and salt.
   - In another bowl, beat together sugar and butter until fluffy. Add eggs one at a time, then stir in rose water and milk.
   - Gradually add the dry ingredients and fold in the ground pistachios.
   - Divide the batter between the pans and bake for 25-30 minutes. Let cool.
2. **Prepare the Frosting:**
   - Beat together cream cheese, butter, powdered sugar, and rose water until smooth. For extra flavor, mix in pistachio paste or ground pistachios.

3. **Assemble the Cake:**
    - Frost the cooled cakes with the rose pistachio cream cheese frosting and garnish with crushed pistachios.

Chocolate Mint Cake

Ingredients

For the Cake:

- 1 ¾ cups (220g) all-purpose flour
- 1 ½ tsp baking powder
- ½ tsp baking soda
- ¼ tsp salt
- 1 cup (200g) granulated sugar
- ½ cup (115g) unsalted butter, softened
- 1 cup (240ml) milk
- 2 large eggs
- 1 tsp vanilla extract
- ½ tsp peppermint extract
- ½ cup (50g) cocoa powder
- 1 cup (120g) mini chocolate chips

For the Frosting:

- 8 oz (225g) cream cheese, softened
- ½ cup (115g) unsalted butter, softened
- 4 cups (480g) powdered sugar
- 1 tsp peppermint extract
- 2 tbsp cocoa powder
- Green food coloring (optional)

Instructions

1. **Prepare the Cake:**
    - Preheat the oven to 350°F (175°C). Grease and line two 9-inch (23cm) round cake pans.
    - In a bowl, whisk together flour, baking powder, baking soda, salt, and cocoa powder.
    - In another bowl, beat together butter and sugar until creamy. Add eggs one at a time, then stir in milk, vanilla extract, and peppermint extract.
    - Gradually add the dry ingredients until combined, then fold in mini chocolate chips.
    - Divide the batter between the pans and bake for 25-30 minutes. Let cool.
2. **Prepare the Frosting:**

    - Beat together cream cheese, butter, powdered sugar, peppermint extract, and cocoa powder until smooth. Add food coloring if desired.
3. **Assemble the Cake:**
    - Frost the cooled cakes with the mint chocolate frosting.

Vanilla Bean and Caramel Cake

Ingredients

For the Cake:

- 2 cups (250g) all-purpose flour
- 1 ½ tsp baking powder
- ¼ tsp salt
- 1 cup (200g) granulated sugar
- ½ cup (115g) unsalted butter, softened
- 2 large eggs
- 1 tsp vanilla bean paste or vanilla extract
- 1 cup (240ml) milk

For the Frosting:

- 1 cup (240g) caramel sauce (store-bought or homemade)
- 8 oz (225g) cream cheese, softened
- ½ cup (115g) unsalted butter, softened
- 4 cups (480g) powdered sugar

Instructions

1. **Prepare the Cake:**
    - Preheat the oven to 350°F (175°C). Grease and line two 9-inch (23cm) round cake pans.
    - In a bowl, whisk together flour, baking powder, and salt.
    - In another bowl, beat together sugar and butter until fluffy. Add eggs one at a time, then stir in vanilla paste and milk.
    - Gradually add the dry ingredients until combined.
    - Divide the batter between the pans and bake for 25-30 minutes. Let cool.
2. **Prepare the Frosting:**
    - Beat together caramel sauce, cream cheese, butter, and powdered sugar until smooth.
3. **Assemble the Cake:**
    - Frost the cooled cakes with the caramel frosting.
    -

Coconut Pineapple Cake

Ingredients

For the Cake:

- 2 cups (250g) all-purpose flour
- 1 ½ tsp baking powder
- ½ tsp baking soda
- ¼ tsp salt
- 1 cup (200g) granulated sugar
- ½ cup (115g) unsalted butter, softened
- 2 large eggs
- 1 tsp vanilla extract
- ½ cup (120ml) coconut milk
- 1 cup (100g) shredded coconut
- 1 cup (120g) crushed pineapple, drained

For the Frosting:

- 8 oz (225g) cream cheese, softened
- ½ cup (115g) unsalted butter, softened
- 4 cups (480g) powdered sugar
- 2 tbsp pineapple juice
- 1 tsp vanilla extract
- Shredded coconut for garnish

Instructions

1. **Prepare the Cake:**
   - Preheat the oven to 350°F (175°C). Grease and line two 9-inch (23cm) round cake pans.
   - In a bowl, whisk together flour, baking powder, baking soda, and salt.
   - In another bowl, beat together sugar and butter until creamy. Add eggs one at a time, then stir in vanilla extract and coconut milk.
   - Gradually add the dry ingredients until combined, then fold in shredded coconut and crushed pineapple.
   - Divide the batter between the pans and bake for 25-30 minutes. Let cool.
2. **Prepare the Frosting:**
   - Beat together cream cheese, butter, powdered sugar, pineapple juice, and vanilla extract until smooth.

3. **Assemble the Cake:**
    - Frost the cooled cakes with the pineapple cream cheese frosting and garnish with shredded coconut.

Toffee Caramel Cake

Ingredients

For the Cake:

- 2 cups (250g) all-purpose flour
- 1 ½ tsp baking powder
- ½ tsp baking soda
- ¼ tsp salt
- 1 cup (200g) granulated sugar
- ½ cup (115g) unsalted butter, softened
- 2 large eggs
- 1 tsp vanilla extract
- 1 cup (240ml) buttermilk
- ½ cup (120g) toffee bits

For the Frosting:

- 1 cup (240ml) heavy cream
- ½ cup (100g) brown sugar
- 1/2 cup (115g) unsalted butter
- 1 ½ cups (180g) powdered sugar
- 1 tsp vanilla extract

Instructions

1. **Prepare the Cake:**
    - Preheat the oven to 350°F (175°C). Grease and line two 9-inch (23cm) round cake pans.
    - In a bowl, whisk together flour, baking powder, baking soda, and salt.
    - In another bowl, beat together sugar and butter until fluffy. Add eggs one at a time, then stir in vanilla extract and buttermilk.
    - Gradually add the dry ingredients until combined, then fold in toffee bits.
    - Divide the batter between the pans and bake for 25-30 minutes. Let cool.
2. **Prepare the Frosting:**
    - In a saucepan, combine heavy cream, brown sugar, and butter over medium heat. Stir until melted and smooth, then bring to a simmer for 5-7 minutes.
    - Remove from heat and whisk in powdered sugar and vanilla extract until smooth.

- Let the frosting cool slightly before using.
3. **Assemble the Cake:**
   - Frost the cooled cakes with the toffee caramel frosting.

Lemon Poppy Seed Cake

Ingredients

For the Cake:

- 2 cups (250g) all-purpose flour
- 1 ½ tsp baking powder
- ½ tsp salt
- 1 cup (200g) granulated sugar
- ½ cup (115g) unsalted butter, softened
- 2 large eggs
- 1 tsp vanilla extract
- 1 tbsp lemon zest
- 2 tbsp poppy seeds
- 1 cup (240ml) buttermilk

For the Frosting:

- 8 oz (225g) cream cheese, softened
- ¼ cup (60g) unsalted butter, softened
- 4 cups (480g) powdered sugar
- 1 tsp vanilla extract
- 2 tbsp fresh lemon juice

Instructions

1. **Prepare the Cake:**
   - Preheat the oven to 350°F (175°C). Grease and line two 9-inch (23cm) round cake pans.
   - In a bowl, whisk together flour, baking powder, and salt.
   - In another bowl, beat together sugar and butter until creamy. Add eggs one at a time, then stir in vanilla extract, lemon zest, and poppy seeds.
   - Gradually add the dry ingredients, alternating with the buttermilk, until combined.
   - Divide the batter between the pans and bake for 25-30 minutes. Let cool.
2. **Prepare the Frosting:**
   - Beat together cream cheese, butter, powdered sugar, vanilla extract, and lemon juice until smooth.
3. **Assemble the Cake:**
   - Frost the cooled cakes with the lemon cream cheese frosting.

Chocolate Orange Cake

Ingredients

For the Cake:

- 2 cups (250g) all-purpose flour
- 1 ½ tsp baking powder
- ½ tsp baking soda
- ¼ tsp salt
- 1 cup (200g) granulated sugar
- ½ cup (115g) unsalted butter, softened
- 2 large eggs
- 1 tsp vanilla extract
- 2 tbsp orange zest
- 1 cup (240ml) orange juice
- ½ cup (50g) cocoa powder

For the Frosting:

- 8 oz (225g) cream cheese, softened
- ½ cup (115g) unsalted butter, softened
- 4 cups (480g) powdered sugar
- 1 tsp vanilla extract
- 2 tbsp fresh orange juice
- Orange zest for garnish

Instructions

1. **Prepare the Cake:**
    - Preheat the oven to 350°F (175°C). Grease and line two 9-inch (23cm) round cake pans.
    - In a bowl, whisk together flour, baking powder, baking soda, salt, and cocoa powder.
    - In another bowl, beat together sugar and butter until creamy. Add eggs one at a time, then stir in vanilla extract and orange zest.
    - Gradually add the dry ingredients, alternating with the orange juice, until combined.
    - Divide the batter between the pans and bake for 25-30 minutes. Let cool.
2. **Prepare the Frosting:**

- Beat together cream cheese, butter, powdered sugar, vanilla extract, and orange juice until smooth.
3. **Assemble the Cake:**
    - Frost the cooled cakes with the orange cream cheese frosting and garnish with orange zest.

Mint Chocolate Chip Cake

Ingredients

For the Cake:

- 2 cups (250g) all-purpose flour
- 1 ½ tsp baking powder
- ½ tsp salt
- 1 cup (200g) granulated sugar
- ½ cup (115g) unsalted butter, softened
- 2 large eggs
- 1 tsp vanilla extract
- 1 tsp mint extract
- ½ cup (120ml) milk
- 1 cup (120g) mini chocolate chips
- Green food coloring (optional)

For the Frosting:

- 8 oz (225g) cream cheese, softened
- ½ cup (115g) unsalted butter, softened
- 4 cups (480g) powdered sugar
- 1 tsp mint extract
- Green food coloring (optional)

Instructions

1. **Prepare the Cake:**
    - Preheat the oven to 350°F (175°C). Grease and line two 9-inch (23cm) round cake pans.
    - In a bowl, whisk together flour, baking powder, and salt.
    - In another bowl, beat together sugar and butter until fluffy. Add eggs one at a time, then stir in vanilla extract, mint extract, and milk.
    - Gradually add the dry ingredients until combined, then fold in mini chocolate chips and a few drops of green food coloring if desired.
    - Divide the batter between the pans and bake for 25-30 minutes. Let cool.
2. **Prepare the Frosting:**
    - Beat together cream cheese, butter, powdered sugar, mint extract, and green food coloring until smooth.
3. **Assemble the Cake:**

    - Frost the cooled cakes with the mint chocolate chip frosting.

Churro Layer Cake

Ingredients

For the Cake:

- 2 cups (250g) all-purpose flour
- 1 ½ tsp baking powder
- ½ tsp baking soda
- ¼ tsp salt
- 1 cup (200g) granulated sugar
- ½ cup (115g) unsalted butter, softened
- 2 large eggs
- 1 tsp vanilla extract
- 1 tbsp ground cinnamon
- 1 cup (240ml) buttermilk

For the Frosting:

- 8 oz (225g) cream cheese, softened
- ½ cup (115g) unsalted butter, softened
- 4 cups (480g) powdered sugar
- 1 tbsp ground cinnamon
- 1 tsp vanilla extract

Instructions

1. **Prepare the Cake:**
    - Preheat the oven to 350°F (175°C). Grease and line two 9-inch (23cm) round cake pans.
    - In a bowl, whisk together flour, baking powder, baking soda, salt, and cinnamon.
    - In another bowl, beat together sugar and butter until creamy. Add eggs one at a time, then stir in vanilla extract and buttermilk.
    - Gradually add the dry ingredients until combined.
    - Divide the batter between the pans and bake for 25-30 minutes. Let cool.
2. **Prepare the Frosting:**
    - Beat together cream cheese, butter, powdered sugar, cinnamon, and vanilla extract until smooth.
3. **Assemble the Cake:**
    - Frost the cooled cakes with the churro frosting.

Chai Spice Layer Cake

Ingredients

For the Cake:

- 2 cups (250g) all-purpose flour
- 1 ½ tsp baking powder
- ½ tsp baking soda
- ¼ tsp salt
- 1 cup (200g) granulated sugar
- ½ cup (115g) unsalted butter, softened
- 2 large eggs
- 1 tsp vanilla extract
- 2 tbsp ground chai spice mix
- 1 cup (240ml) buttermilk

For the Frosting:

- 8 oz (225g) cream cheese, softened
- ½ cup (115g) unsalted butter, softened
- 4 cups (480g) powdered sugar
- 1 tsp vanilla extract
- 1 tsp chai spice mix

Instructions

1. **Prepare the Cake:**
    - Preheat the oven to 350°F (175°C). Grease and line two 9-inch (23cm) round cake pans.
    - In a bowl, whisk together flour, baking powder, baking soda, salt, and chai spice mix.
    - In another bowl, beat together sugar and butter until creamy. Add eggs one at a time, then stir in vanilla extract and buttermilk.
    - Gradually add the dry ingredients until combined.
    - Divide the batter between the pans and bake for 25-30 minutes. Let cool.
2. **Prepare the Frosting:**
    - Beat together cream cheese, butter, powdered sugar, vanilla extract, and chai spice mix until smooth.
3. **Assemble the Cake:**
    - Frost the cooled cakes with the chai-spiced frosting.

Dulce de Leche Cake

Ingredients

For the Cake:

- 2 cups (250g) all-purpose flour
- 1 ½ tsp baking powder
- ½ tsp baking soda
- ¼ tsp salt
- 1 cup (200g) granulated sugar
- ½ cup (115g) unsalted butter, softened
- 2 large eggs
- 1 tsp vanilla extract
- 1 cup (240ml) buttermilk
- ½ cup (120g) dulce de leche

For the Frosting:

- 1 cup (240ml) heavy cream
- 1 cup (240g) dulce de leche

Instructions

1. **Prepare the Cake:**
    - Preheat the oven to 350°F (175°C). Grease and line two 9-inch (23cm) round cake pans.
    - In a bowl, whisk together flour, baking powder, baking soda, and salt.
    - In another bowl, beat together sugar and butter until creamy. Add eggs one at a time, then stir in vanilla extract and buttermilk.
    - Gradually add the dry ingredients until combined, then fold in dulce de leche.
    - Divide the batter between the pans and bake for 25-30 minutes. Let cool.
2. **Prepare the Frosting:**
    - In a saucepan, heat the heavy cream and dulce de leche together until warm and combined.
    - Let cool slightly before frosting.
3. **Assemble the Cake:**
    - Frost the cooled cakes with the dulce de leche frosting.

Bourbon Pecan Cake

Ingredients

For the Cake:

- 2 cups (250g) all-purpose flour
- 1 ½ tsp baking powder
- ½ tsp baking soda
- ¼ tsp salt
- 1 cup (200g) granulated sugar
- ½ cup (115g) unsalted butter, softened
- 3 large eggs
- 1 tsp vanilla extract
- 1/4 cup (60ml) bourbon
- 1 cup (240ml) buttermilk
- 1 cup (120g) chopped pecans

For the Frosting:

- 8 oz (225g) cream cheese, softened
- ½ cup (115g) unsalted butter, softened
- 4 cups (480g) powdered sugar
- 1 tsp vanilla extract
- 1/4 cup (60ml) bourbon
- ½ cup (60g) chopped pecans (for garnish)

Instructions

1. **Prepare the Cake:**
    - Preheat the oven to 350°F (175°C). Grease and line two 9-inch (23cm) round cake pans.
    - In a bowl, whisk together flour, baking powder, baking soda, and salt.
    - In another bowl, beat together sugar and butter until creamy. Add eggs one at a time, then stir in vanilla extract and bourbon.
    - Gradually add the dry ingredients until combined. Add buttermilk and fold in chopped pecans.
    - Divide the batter between the pans and bake for 25-30 minutes. Let cool.
2. **Prepare the Frosting:**
    - Beat together cream cheese, butter, powdered sugar, vanilla extract, and bourbon until smooth.

3. **Assemble the Cake:**
    - Frost the cooled cakes with the bourbon pecan frosting, and garnish with chopped pecans.

Cookies and Cream Cake

Ingredients

For the Cake:

- 2 cups (250g) all-purpose flour
- 1 ½ tsp baking powder
- ½ tsp baking soda
- ¼ tsp salt
- 1 cup (200g) granulated sugar
- ½ cup (115g) unsalted butter, softened
- 2 large eggs
- 1 tsp vanilla extract
- 1 cup (240ml) buttermilk
- 1 cup (100g) crushed chocolate sandwich cookies (Oreos)

For the Frosting:

- 8 oz (225g) cream cheese, softened
- ½ cup (115g) unsalted butter, softened
- 4 cups (480g) powdered sugar
- 1 tsp vanilla extract
- 1 cup (100g) crushed chocolate sandwich cookies (Oreos)

Instructions

1. **Prepare the Cake:**
    - Preheat the oven to 350°F (175°C). Grease and line two 9-inch (23cm) round cake pans.
    - In a bowl, whisk together flour, baking powder, baking soda, and salt.
    - In another bowl, beat together sugar and butter until creamy. Add eggs one at a time, then stir in vanilla extract and buttermilk.
    - Gradually add the dry ingredients until combined, then fold in crushed cookies.
    - Divide the batter between the pans and bake for 25-30 minutes. Let cool.
2. **Prepare the Frosting:**
    - Beat together cream cheese, butter, powdered sugar, vanilla extract, and crushed cookies until smooth.
3. **Assemble the Cake:**
    - Frost the cooled cakes with the cookies and cream frosting.

Key Lime Pie Cake

Ingredients

For the Cake:

- 2 cups (250g) all-purpose flour
- 1 ½ tsp baking powder
- ½ tsp baking soda
- ¼ tsp salt
- 1 cup (200g) granulated sugar
- ½ cup (115g) unsalted butter, softened
- 3 large eggs
- 1 tsp vanilla extract
- ½ cup (120ml) fresh key lime juice
- 1 cup (240ml) buttermilk

For the Frosting:

- 8 oz (225g) cream cheese, softened
- ½ cup (115g) unsalted butter, softened
- 4 cups (480g) powdered sugar
- 1 tsp vanilla extract
- ¼ cup (60ml) fresh key lime juice
- Zest of 2 key limes

Instructions

1. **Prepare the Cake:**
   - Preheat the oven to 350°F (175°C). Grease and line two 9-inch (23cm) round cake pans.
   - In a bowl, whisk together flour, baking powder, baking soda, and salt.
   - In another bowl, beat together sugar and butter until creamy. Add eggs one at a time, then stir in vanilla extract and key lime juice.
   - Gradually add the dry ingredients until combined, then mix in buttermilk.
   - Divide the batter between the pans and bake for 25-30 minutes. Let cool.
2. **Prepare the Frosting:**
   - Beat together cream cheese, butter, powdered sugar, vanilla extract, key lime juice, and zest until smooth.
3. **Assemble the Cake:**
   - Frost the cooled cakes with the key lime frosting.

Apple Cinnamon Cake

Ingredients

For the Cake:

- 2 cups (250g) all-purpose flour
- 1 ½ tsp baking powder
- ½ tsp baking soda
- 1 tsp ground cinnamon
- ¼ tsp salt
- 1 cup (200g) granulated sugar
- ½ cup (115g) unsalted butter, softened
- 2 large eggs
- 1 tsp vanilla extract
- 1 cup (240ml) buttermilk
- 1 ½ cups (180g) chopped apples (preferably Granny Smith)

For the Frosting:

- 8 oz (225g) cream cheese, softened
- ½ cup (115g) unsalted butter, softened
- 4 cups (480g) powdered sugar
- 1 tsp vanilla extract
- 1 tsp ground cinnamon

Instructions

1. **Prepare the Cake:**
    - Preheat the oven to 350°F (175°C). Grease and line two 9-inch (23cm) round cake pans.
    - In a bowl, whisk together flour, baking powder, baking soda, cinnamon, and salt.
    - In another bowl, beat together sugar and butter until creamy. Add eggs one at a time, then stir in vanilla extract.
    - Gradually add the dry ingredients until combined, then fold in chopped apples and buttermilk.
    - Divide the batter between the pans and bake for 25-30 minutes. Let cool.
2. **Prepare the Frosting:**
    - Beat together cream cheese, butter, powdered sugar, vanilla extract, and cinnamon until smooth.

3. **Assemble the Cake:**
    - Frost the cooled cakes with the apple cinnamon frosting.

Cherry Almond Cake

Ingredients

For the Cake:

- 2 cups (250g) all-purpose flour
- 1 ½ tsp baking powder
- ½ tsp baking soda
- ¼ tsp salt
- 1 cup (200g) granulated sugar
- ½ cup (115g) unsalted butter, softened
- 2 large eggs
- 1 tsp vanilla extract
- 1 tsp almond extract
- 1 cup (240ml) buttermilk
- 1 cup (120g) maraschino cherries, chopped

For the Frosting:

- 8 oz (225g) cream cheese, softened
- ½ cup (115g) unsalted butter, softened
- 4 cups (480g) powdered sugar
- 1 tsp vanilla extract
- 1 tsp almond extract
- ½ cup (50g) chopped maraschino cherries

Instructions

1. **Prepare the Cake:**
    - Preheat the oven to 350°F (175°C). Grease and line two 9-inch (23cm) round cake pans.
    - In a bowl, whisk together flour, baking powder, baking soda, and salt.
    - In another bowl, beat together sugar and butter until creamy. Add eggs one at a time, then stir in vanilla and almond extracts.
    - Gradually add the dry ingredients until combined, then fold in chopped cherries and buttermilk.
    - Divide the batter between the pans and bake for 25-30 minutes. Let cool.
2. **Prepare the Frosting:**
    - Beat together cream cheese, butter, powdered sugar, vanilla extract, almond extract, and chopped cherries until smooth.

3. **Assemble the Cake:**
    - Frost the cooled cakes with the cherry almond frosting.

Cherry Blossom Cake

Ingredients

For the Cake:

- 2 cups (250g) all-purpose flour
- 1 ½ tsp baking powder
- ½ tsp baking soda
- ¼ tsp salt
- 1 cup (200g) granulated sugar
- ½ cup (115g) unsalted butter, softened
- 2 large eggs
- 1 tsp vanilla extract
- 1 tsp almond extract
- 1 cup (240ml) buttermilk
- ½ cup (80g) maraschino cherries, chopped

For the Frosting:

- 8 oz (225g) cream cheese, softened
- ½ cup (115g) unsalted butter, softened
- 4 cups (480g) powdered sugar
- 1 tsp vanilla extract
- 1 tsp almond extract
- Pink food coloring
- ½ cup (50g) chopped maraschino cherries for garnish

Instructions

1. **Prepare the Cake:**
    - Preheat the oven to 350°F (175°C). Grease and line two 9-inch (23cm) round cake pans.
    - In a bowl, whisk together flour, baking powder, baking soda, and salt.
    - In another bowl, beat together sugar and butter until creamy. Add eggs one at a time, then stir in vanilla and almond extracts.
    - Gradually add the dry ingredients until combined, then fold in chopped cherries and buttermilk.
    - Divide the batter between the pans and bake for 25-30 minutes. Let cool.
2. **Prepare the Frosting:**

- Beat together cream cheese, butter, powdered sugar, vanilla extract, almond extract, and a few drops of pink food coloring until smooth.
3. **Assemble the Cake:**
    - Frost the cooled cakes with the cherry blossom frosting and garnish with chopped cherries.

Gingerbread Spice Cake

Ingredients

For the Cake:

- 2 ½ cups (312g) all-purpose flour
- 2 tsp ground ginger
- 1 ½ tsp ground cinnamon
- 1 tsp ground cloves
- ½ tsp ground nutmeg
- 1 ½ tsp baking soda
- ¼ tsp salt
- ¾ cup (150g) granulated sugar
- ½ cup (100g) brown sugar, packed
- ½ cup (115g) unsalted butter, softened
- 2 large eggs
- 1 cup (240ml) buttermilk
- ½ cup (120ml) molasses
- 1 tsp vanilla extract

For the Frosting:

- 8 oz (225g) cream cheese, softened
- ½ cup (115g) unsalted butter, softened
- 4 cups (480g) powdered sugar
- 1 tsp vanilla extract
- 1 tsp ground cinnamon

Instructions

1. **Prepare the Cake:**
    - Preheat the oven to 350°F (175°C). Grease and line two 9-inch (23cm) round cake pans.
    - In a bowl, whisk together flour, ginger, cinnamon, cloves, nutmeg, baking soda, and salt.
    - In a separate bowl, beat together sugar, brown sugar, and butter until creamy. Add eggs one at a time.
    - Mix in buttermilk, molasses, and vanilla. Gradually add the dry ingredients until combined.
    - Divide the batter between the pans and bake for 25-30 minutes. Let cool.

2. **Prepare the Frosting:**
   - Beat together cream cheese, butter, powdered sugar, vanilla, and cinnamon until smooth.
3. **Assemble the Cake:**
   - Frost the cooled cakes with the cream cheese frosting.

Blueberry Cream Cheese Cake

Ingredients

For the Cake:

- 2 cups (250g) all-purpose flour
- 1 ½ tsp baking powder
- ½ tsp baking soda
- ¼ tsp salt
- 1 cup (200g) granulated sugar
- ½ cup (115g) unsalted butter, softened
- 3 large eggs
- 1 tsp vanilla extract
- 1 cup (240ml) sour cream
- 1 ½ cups (150g) fresh blueberries

For the Frosting:

- 8 oz (225g) cream cheese, softened
- ½ cup (115g) unsalted butter, softened
- 4 cups (480g) powdered sugar
- 1 tsp vanilla extract
- ¼ cup (60ml) heavy cream

Instructions

1. **Prepare the Cake:**
     - Preheat the oven to 350°F (175°C). Grease and line two 9-inch (23cm) round cake pans.
     - In a bowl, whisk together flour, baking powder, baking soda, and salt.
     - In another bowl, beat together sugar and butter until creamy. Add eggs one at a time, then stir in vanilla extract.
     - Gradually add the dry ingredients and mix in sour cream. Fold in blueberries gently.
     - Divide the batter between the pans and bake for 25-30 minutes. Let cool.
2. **Prepare the Frosting:**
     - Beat together cream cheese, butter, powdered sugar, vanilla extract, and heavy cream until smooth.
3. **Assemble the Cake:**
     - Frost the cooled cakes with the blueberry cream cheese frosting.

Maple Brown Sugar Cake

Ingredients

For the Cake:

- 2 ½ cups (312g) all-purpose flour
- 1 ½ tsp baking powder
- ½ tsp baking soda
- ¼ tsp salt
- 1 cup (200g) brown sugar, packed
- ½ cup (115g) unsalted butter, softened
- 3 large eggs
- 1 tsp vanilla extract
- 1 cup (240ml) buttermilk
- ½ cup (120ml) pure maple syrup

For the Frosting:

- 8 oz (225g) cream cheese, softened
- ½ cup (115g) unsalted butter, softened
- 4 cups (480g) powdered sugar
- 1 tsp vanilla extract
- 3 tbsp maple syrup

Instructions

1. **Prepare the Cake:**
    - Preheat the oven to 350°F (175°C). Grease and line two 9-inch (23cm) round cake pans.
    - In a bowl, whisk together flour, baking powder, baking soda, and salt.
    - In another bowl, beat together brown sugar and butter until creamy. Add eggs one at a time, then stir in vanilla extract.
    - Gradually add the dry ingredients, alternating with buttermilk and maple syrup.
    - Divide the batter between the pans and bake for 25-30 minutes. Let cool.
2. **Prepare the Frosting:**
    - Beat together cream cheese, butter, powdered sugar, vanilla extract, and maple syrup until smooth.
3. **Assemble the Cake:**
    - Frost the cooled cakes with the maple brown sugar frosting.

Tropical Mango Coconut Cake

Ingredients

For the Cake:

- 2 cups (250g) all-purpose flour
- 1 ½ tsp baking powder
- ½ tsp baking soda
- ¼ tsp salt
- 1 cup (200g) granulated sugar
- ½ cup (115g) unsalted butter, softened
- 3 large eggs
- 1 tsp vanilla extract
- ½ cup (120ml) coconut milk
- ½ cup (120g) mango puree
- 1 cup (80g) shredded coconut

For the Frosting:

- 8 oz (225g) cream cheese, softened
- ½ cup (115g) unsalted butter, softened
- 4 cups (480g) powdered sugar
- 1 tsp vanilla extract
- 1/4 cup (60ml) coconut milk

Instructions

1. **Prepare the Cake:**
   - Preheat the oven to 350°F (175°C). Grease and line two 9-inch (23cm) round cake pans.
   - In a bowl, whisk together flour, baking powder, baking soda, and salt.
   - In another bowl, beat together sugar and butter until creamy. Add eggs one at a time, then stir in vanilla extract.
   - Gradually add the dry ingredients, alternating with coconut milk and mango puree. Fold in shredded coconut.
   - Divide the batter between the pans and bake for 25-30 minutes. Let cool.
2. **Prepare the Frosting:**
   - Beat together cream cheese, butter, powdered sugar, vanilla extract, and coconut milk until smooth.
3. **Assemble the Cake:**

- Frost the cooled cakes with the tropical mango coconut frosting.